My Manners

By

Grace Jones

Crabtree Publishing Company
www.crabtreebooks.com
1-800-387-7650

Published in Canada
Crabtree Publishing
616 Welland Avenue
St. Catharines, ON
L2M 5V6

Published in the United States
Crabtree Publishing
PMB 59051
350 Fifth Ave, 59th Floor
New York, NY 10118

Published by Crabtree Publishing Company in 2017

First Published by Book Life in 2016
Copyright © 2017 Book Life

Author
Grace Jones

Editors
Grace Jones
Janine Deschenes

Design
Danielle Jones

Proofreader
Crystal Sikkens

Production coordinator and
prepress technician (interior)
Margaret Amy Salter

Prepress technician (covers)
Ken Wright

Print coordinator
Katherine Berti

Printed in Hong Kong/012017/BK20161024

Photographs

Bigstock: © style-photographs, p5; © famveldman, p8;
Dreamstime: © Serban Enache, p20
Thinkstock: © szefei, p9

All other images from Shutterstock

Library and Archives Canada Cataloguing in Publication

Jones, Grace, 1990-, author
        My manners / Grace Jones.

(Our values)
Issued in print and electronic formats.
ISBN 978-0-7787-3260-0 (hardback).--
ISBN 978-0-7787-3309-6 (paperback).--
ISBN 978-1-4271-1891-2 (html)

        1. Courtesy--Juvenile literature. 2. Etiquette for children
and teenagers--Juvenile literature. I. Title.

BJ1857.C5J66 2016   j395.1'22   C2016-906653-3
                                               C2016-906867-6

Library of Congress Cataloging-in-Publication Data

CIP available at Library of Congress

Contents

Words that look like **this** can be found in the glossary on page 24.

What are Manners?

Manners are the ways people behave at different times and in different places.

Manners can be good or bad. You should always try to have good manners.

Good Manners

If you have good manners, you are **polite** and show **respect** toward other people.

If you ask someone for something, always say "please."

Say "thank you" when someone gives you something. It is also important to say "thank you" when someone helps you.

I am sorry I hurt your feelings.

If you hurt or upset someone, you should always say sorry.

9

At Home

Take off your shoes when you get inside your house.

Shut the door quietly, too!

Do not shout loudly. Other people in your family may want quiet.

11

Put all your toys away when you have finished playing with them.

Dinner Time

Have you washed your hands?

Wash your hands before every meal and after you use the bathroom.

Use a knife, fork, and spoon to eat your food.

Do not speak with food in your mouth.

Chew your food with your mouth closed.

16

Would you like a napkin to wipe your mouth?

Use a napkin to wipe your mouth.

Out and About

Excuse me, I need to get by.

Say "excuse me" if you need to pass by someone. Never push.

Put your trash in the garbage. Do not leave it for someone else to pick up.

Hold the door open for the next person.

What time is it?

Do not be late when you are meeting your friends.

At School

Be quiet and listen when others are talking.
Raise your hand when you want to speak.

Always try to help someone if they need it.

Glossary

parents Moms and dads

polite Having good manners or showing respect for other people

respect A feeling that someone or something is good and important

Index